The Right Way to Love a Bipolar Person

A Practical Guide to Understanding, Compassion, and Support

Rachel J. Oles

Table of Contents

Chapter 1

BIPOLAR BASICS

Bipolar disorder is a complex and often misunderstood mental health issue that affects millions of individuals worldwide. It's marked by large and often unpredictable mood fluctuations, which can have a tremendous impact on a person's life, relationships, and general well-being.

To comprehend bipolar disease, it's vital to grasp the notion of the bipolar spectrum, the numerous forms of bipolar disorder, and the prevalent symptoms and warning signals linked with the condition.

The Bipolar Spectrum

The bipolar spectrum is a conceptual framework that helps us understand the varied variety of mood disorders that come under the bipolar umbrella.

Instead of considering bipolar illness as a one-size-fits-all diagnosis, the spectrum accepts that people might experience a wide diversity of mood episodes, from severe depression to strong mania, and everything in between.

The bipolar spectrum often comprises the following key elements:

1. **Bipolar I disease:** This is the classic form of bipolar disease and is characterized by episodes of mania and depression. Manic episodes can be severe and debilitating, often leading to reckless behavior, whereas depressed periods are distinguished by great despair and hopelessness.

2. **Bipolar II Disorder:** Bipolar II is characterized by periodic episodes of depression and hypomania, a milder form of

mania. Hypomanic episodes are less severe than full-blown mania and may involve enhanced energy and creativity.

3. **<u>Cyclothymic disease:</u>** This is a milder form of bipolar disease, with cyclical mood swings that are less severe than those in Bipolar I and II. People with cyclothymic disorder may experience chronic mood instability but don't satisfy the threshold for full depressed or manic episodes.

4. **<u>Other Specified and Unspecified Bipolar Disorders:</u>** Sometimes, individuals encounter symptoms that don't neatly fall into the existing categories. Clinicians may use these classifications when the presentation of bipolar symptoms is atypical.

Types of Bipolar Disorder

Within the bipolar spectrum, there are multiple distinct forms of bipolar disorder, each characterized by specific patterns of mood episodes. These include:

1. Bipolar I Disorder:

- Description: Bipolar I disease is considered the standard form of bipolar disease. It is characterized by manic periods, which can be severe and debilitating, and depressed episodes.

- Manic Episodes: Mania is the defining feature of Bipolar I Disorder. During manic episodes, individuals may experience heightened energy, exhilaration, racing thoughts, increased activity, decreased desire for sleep, grandiosity, and impulsive behavior. These symptoms can profoundly affect daily life and relationships.

- <u>Depressive Episodes:</u> Depressive episodes in Bipolar I Disorder are comparable to those in major depressive disorder, distinguished by severe sorrow, lack of interest or pleasure, changes in eating and sleep habits, exhaustion, and thoughts of hopelessness.

2. Bipolar II Disorder:

- <u>Description:</u> Bipolar II Disorder entails periodic bouts of significant depression and hypomania. Hypomania is a milder version of mania marked by increased energy, creativity, and activity.

- <u>Hypomanic Episodes:</u> Hypomania is less severe than mania, and persons with Bipolar II Disorder often maintain a level of functionality during these episodes. They may feel more productive, and communicative, and have an improved mood.

- <u>Depressive Episodes:</u> Depressive episodes in Bipolar II Disorder are comparable to those in Bipolar I and major depressive disorder. They involve feelings of misery, worthlessness, and despair.

3. Cyclothymic Disorder:

- <u>Description:</u> Cyclothymic disease is a milder variant of bipolar disease, characterized by chronic mood instability. Individuals with this illness suffer numerous bouts of hypomanic and depressive symptoms that do not match the criteria for full manic or depressive episodes.

- <u>Chronic Mood Swings:</u> The mood swings in Cyclothymic Disorder are less severe than in other forms but are continuous and ongoing. These mood fluctuations might influence daily functioning and relationships.

4. Rapid Cycling Bipolar Disorder:

- Description: Rapid Cycling Bipolar Disorder is not a different type but a specifier that can be applied to Bipolar I or Bipolar II. It is characterized by experiencing four or more mood episodes (manic, hypomanic, depressive, or mixed) within a year.

- Frequent Mood transitions: People with rapid cycling may experience rapid and often unpredictable transitions between manic and depressed states, making their illness tougher to control.

5. Mixed Features Bipolar Disorder:

- Description: Mixed Features Bipolar Disorder is defined by the occurrence of both manic or hypomanic symptoms and depression symptoms simultaneously or in fast succession.

- <u>Complex Mood States:</u> Individuals with mixed features may experience the excitement, restlessness, or impulsivity of mania alongside the sadness and hopelessness of depression. This combination might lead to significant emotional distress.

6. Other Specified and Unspecified Bipolar Disorders:

- <u>Description:</u> In some circumstances, individuals may not cleanly fit into the defined categories of bipolar disorder. Clinicians may utilize the "Other Specified Bipolar Disorder" or "Unspecified Bipolar Disorder" classifications when the presentation of bipolar symptoms is atypical or doesn't correspond with the particular criteria for the known forms.

<u>Common Symptoms and Warning Signs</u>

Recognizing the symptoms and warning signs of bipolar disorder is critical for early diagnosis and intervention. While individuals with bipolar disorder can have diverse experiences, some typical symptoms and warning indicators include:

1. <u>Extreme Mood Swings:</u> Individuals may experience tremendous highs (mania or hypomania) and lows (depression) that disturb their daily life.

2. <u>Changes in Energy Levels:</u> During manic or hypomanic episodes, energy levels may rise, resulting in greater activity and a reduced need for sleep. Depressive episodes are generally defined by excessive weariness and lethargy.

3. <u>Changes in Sleep Patterns:</u> Insomnia during manic episodes and excessive sleep during depressed episodes are typical.

4. <u>Irritability:</u> Increased irritability and mood volatility can be prominent.

5. <u>Impulsivity:</u> Manic episodes can lead to impulsive and risky conduct, such as excessive spending or substance addiction.

6. <u>Decreased Interest or Pleasure:</u> Individuals may lose interest in activities they once enjoyed, even during moments of mania.

7. <u>Difficulty Concentrating:</u> Both manic and depressive periods can affect cognitive function and focus.

8. <u>Changes in Appetite and Weight:</u> Appetite variations and weight changes are frequent during mood episodes.

9. <u>Social Isolation:</u> Individuals with bipolar disorder may withdraw from social contacts during depressed periods.

10. Suicidal Thoughts: Severe depression episodes may include thoughts of self-harm or suicide.

Understanding the bipolar spectrum, the numerous types of bipolar illness, and the typical symptoms and warning indications are vital for offering support and seeking appropriate treatment for persons living with this condition. It's important to remember that bipolar disorder is a highly treatable diagnosis, and with the correct support and care, individuals may lead fulfilling lives.

Chapter 2

<u>COMMON MYTHS AROUND BIPOLAR DISORDER</u>

Bipolar disorder is a complex and often misunderstood mental health issue. Unfortunately, various myths and misconceptions surround bipolar disease, contributing to stigma and making it difficult for those affected to seek assistance and receive the care they need. Let's review some of the most frequent beliefs regarding bipolar disease and dispel them with accurate information:

<u>Myth 1: Bipolar Disorder is Just Moodiness</u>

<u>Reality:</u> Bipolar disorder is not ordinary moodiness or periodic mood changes. It is a significant mental health illness marked by extreme and frequently unpredictable fluctuations in mood. While everyone experiences mood fluctuations, bipolar illness entails acute, protracted periods of depression, mania, or hypomania that profoundly affect a person's life.

Myth 2: People with Bipolar Disorder Are Violent and Dangerous

Reality: People with bipolar disorder are not inherently aggressive or dangerous. The great majority of individuals with bipolar disorder are more likely to damage themselves than others. Proper therapy and support can help regulate mood swings and limit the chance of any harm.

Myth 3: Bipolar Disorder is Rare

Reality: Bipolar disorder is not rare. It impacts millions of individuals worldwide. According to the World Health Organization, it is one of the top 20 main causes of disability globally. However, it often goes untreated or misdiagnosed, contributing to the impression of its rarity.

Myth 4: Bipolar Disorder is Just a Lack of Self-Control

Reality: Bipolar disorder is not a sign of weakness or a lack of self-control. It is a complicated neurological disorder with genetic, biochemical, and environmental elements at play. People with bipolar disorder cannot simply "snap out of it."

Myth 5: Bipolar Disorder Only Affects Mood

Reality: Bipolar disorder does alter mood, but it can also damage cognitive performance, energy levels, sleep patterns, and more. It can lead to interruptions in daily life and relationships, impacting work, school, and social activities.

Myth 6: Everyone with Bipolar Disorder Has Extreme Mood Swings

Reality: While dramatic mood fluctuations are a hallmark of bipolar disease, not everyone experiences them to the same degree. Some individuals may have lesser versions of the ailment, such as Bipolar II or cyclothymic disorder, which include less severe mood episodes.

Myth 7: Medication Is the Only Treatment for Bipolar Disorder

Reality: Medication can be a crucial element of managing bipolar disorder, but it is not the only treatment. Therapy, lifestyle modifications, and a strong support system also play key roles in controlling the illness. Treatment plans should be tailored and may include a combination of treatments.

Myth 8: People with Bipolar Disorder Cannot Lead Fulfilling Lives

Reality: With adequate treatment and support, persons with bipolar disorder can have full and productive lives. Many persons with bipolar disorder flourish in their occupations, maintain stable relationships, and contribute positively to their communities.

Myth 9: Bipolar Disorder Affects Only Young People

Reality: Bipolar disorder can develop at any age, from childhood through late adulthood. While it frequently shows in late adolescence or early adulthood, some individuals are not diagnosed until later in life.

Myth 10: Everyone with Bipolar Disorder Exhibits Identical Symptoms

Reality: Bipolar disorder is a highly varied condition. Each person may suffer distinct combinations of symptoms, with variable levels of severity. Additionally, the course of the illness might fluctuate substantially from one individual to another.

Myth 11: Bipolar Disorder Can Be Cured

Reality: Bipolar disorder is a chronic condition, and there is no recognized cure. However, with the correct treatment, many individuals can achieve long periods of stability and effectively manage their symptoms. Treatment often combines medication, therapy, and lifestyle adjustments to maintain a stable, healthy existence.

Myth 12: Bipolar Disorder is Just a "Label"

Reality: While a diagnosis of bipolar disorder is a label, it serves a significant role. It helps individuals and healthcare providers understand and treat the illness efficiently. Receiving a diagnosis can lead to access to appropriate therapy, support, and knowledge about the disease.

Myth 13: Bipolar Disorder is the Same as Borderline Personality Disorder (BPD)

Reality: Bipolar disorder and borderline personality disorder are distinct diseases with different diagnostic criteria and treatments. Bipolar disorder is usually defined by mood episodes, while BPD is characterized by emotional instability, impulsivity, and difficulty in interpersonal interactions. It is crucial to differentiate between the two for accurate diagnosis and therapy.

Myth 14: People with Bipolar Disorder Should Avoid Stress at All Costs

Reality: While stress can induce mood episodes in people with bipolar disorder, it is not feasible or beneficial to avoid stress. Learning to handle stress through coping methods, therapy, and lifestyle improvements is a more practical approach.

Myth 15: You Can Always Spot Bipolar Disorder by Someone's Behavior

Reality: Not everyone with bipolar disorder exhibits outward indicators of their condition. Many individuals can disguise their symptoms or manage them well in public. Additionally, the expression of bipolar disorder can vary widely, making it difficult to recognize in certain circumstances.

Myth 16: You Can't Help Someone with Bipolar Disorder

Reality: You can undoubtedly help someone with bipolar disorder. Support from loved ones, friends, and specialists is crucial to managing the disease efficiently. This support can involve promoting therapy, providing a listening ear, and offering aid during difficult moments.

Myth 17: People with Bipolar Disorder Are Always Creatives or Geniuses

Reality: While there is a correlation between bipolar disorder and creativity in some circumstances, not all individuals with bipolar disorder are highly creative or genius-level intellects. The link between creativity and bipolar disorder is complex and varies among individuals.

Myth 18: People with Bipolar Disorder Are Attention-Seeking

Reality: The mood episodes and actions shown by individuals with bipolar disorder are not driven by a need for attention. They are a result of the neurobiological and psychosocial aspects linked with the illness.

Myth 19: People with Bipolar Disorder Are Unreliable

Reality: While bipolar disease can provide obstacles, many persons with the condition lead highly successful and reliable lives. Treatment, support, and self-management strategies enable people to retain stability and meet their commitments.

Myth 20: Bipolar Disorder is the Same for Everyone

Reality: Bipolar disorder is a very individualized condition. No two people will experience it the same way. Factors like the kind of bipolar illness, severity of symptoms, and other co-occurring diseases all contribute to the unique experience of the disorder for each individual.

Challenging these stereotypes and sharing factual information about bipolar disease is vital for decreasing stigma, enhancing understanding, and encouraging those affected to seek appropriate assistance. Education, open discussion, and empathy are critical steps toward providing improved support and care for persons living with bipolar disease.

Chapter 3

<u>THE DIAGNOSIS PROCESS</u>

The diagnostic procedure of bipolar disorder entails a thorough evaluation by a skilled healthcare practitioner, generally a psychiatrist or clinical psychologist. It's vital to obtain a proper diagnosis because this condition can greatly disrupt a person's life, and the right treatment plan can make a huge difference in controlling symptoms and increasing overall well-being. Here's an in-depth look at the diagnosing procedure for bipolar disorder:

1. Clinical Assessment:

- <u>Initial Evaluation:</u> The diagnosis process frequently begins with an initial examination where the individual presents their symptoms, medical history, and any family history of mood disorders. It's crucial to offer the healthcare expert with as much information as possible.

- <u>Clinical Interview:</u> A detailed clinical interview is undertaken to analyze the individual's present and prior symptoms. This includes an exploration of mood episodes, their duration, frequency, and severity, as well as any accompanying aspects such as changes in sleep habits, energy levels, and behavior.

2. Differential Diagnosis:
- The healthcare practitioner must rule out other disorders that can mimic bipolar disorder. This involves distinguishing it from unipolar depression, other mood disorders, substance addiction, and physical illnesses that can affect mood.

3. Mood Assessment:
- The doctor will utilize established criteria to assess the presence of manic or

hypomanic episodes (for Bipolar I and Bipolar II illnesses) and depressive episodes.

- For a diagnosis of Bipolar I Disorder, the individual must have experienced at least one manic episode. A diagnosis of Bipolar II Disorder needs at least one hypomanic and one depressed episode.

4. Family History:
- The presence of bipolar illness or other mood disorders in the family might be an important element in the diagnostic process, as there is a genetic component to bipolar disorder.

5. Timeline of Episodes:
- The diagnostic method frequently entails a comprehensive evaluation of the timeline of mood episodes. This can assist in

establishing the presence and pattern of manic, hypomanic, and depressive episodes.

6. Diagnostic Criteria:

- The diagnostic criteria employed by healthcare professionals are often based on standardized standards such as the Diagnostic and Statistical Manual of Mental Disorders (DSM) or the International Classification of Diseases (ICD). These criteria give a clear foundation for recognizing and diagnosing bipolar illnesses.

7. Rating Scales and Questionnaires:

- In some circumstances, clinicians may utilize rating scales and questionnaires to assess the intensity of symptoms and follow changes over time. For example, the Young Mania Rating Scale (YMRS) and the Hamilton Depression Rating Scale (HAM-D) can provide further information.

8. Medical and Psychological Evaluation:
- A full medical and psychological evaluation is needed to rule out any underlying medical illnesses or substance misuse concerns that may be contributing to the mood changes. This can include blood testing and a physical examination.

9. Self-Reported Questionnaires:
- In some circumstances, individuals may be asked to complete self-reported questionnaires aimed to assess their mood, behavior, and overall mental health. These surveys can be beneficial in providing additional information to aid in the diagnosis.

10. Collateral Information:

- Collateral information from family members or close friends can provide useful insights into the individual's behavior and mood patterns, especially when the individual may not be aware of or willing to reveal their symptoms.

11. Mood and Symptom Tracking:

- Keeping a mood and symptom notebook can help individuals and their healthcare professionals track mood episodes, triggers, and responses to treatment. This information can be important for the continued care of bipolar disorder.

12. Ongoing Evaluation:

- The diagnostic process is not a one-time event but an ongoing review of mood patterns and treatment success. Over time, revisions to the diagnosis or treatment plan may be necessary based on the individual's reaction to treatment and changes in symptoms.

13. Observation and Monitoring:

- In some situations, the healthcare professional may choose to follow and monitor the individual over an extended period, particularly if they suspect a bipolar diagnosis but have not yet experienced the essential mood episodes to confirm it. This technique can assist in ensuring a more accurate diagnosis by collecting the complete range of the illness.

14. Subtyping and Specifying:

- The diagnosis process may involve subtyping and defining the exact kind and symptoms of bipolar disorder. This involves establishing whether it's Bipolar I or Bipolar II, whether it has rapid cycling or mixed features, and whether there are any co-occurring disorders or concerns like substance misuse.

15. Collaboration with Mental Health Professionals:

- Often, the diagnosis of bipolar disorder entails collaboration between several mental health specialists, including psychiatrists, psychologists, and clinical social workers. Each specialist may lend their skills to the diagnostic procedure.

16. Cultural and Societal Considerations:

- It's crucial to explore cultural and socioeconomic elements that may influence the manifestation of bipolar symptoms. Cultural variances in how emotions and behaviors are viewed might alter the diagnosis process, and physicians need to be sensitive to these factors.

17. Informed Consent:

- It's crucial to ensure that the individual being evaluated is informed about the diagnostic process and consents to it. This comprises discussing the objective of the assessment, the nature of the condition, and the available treatment options.

18. Discussion and Education:

- As part of the diagnostic process, the healthcare practitioner often discusses the diagnosis, treatment options, and the course of bipolar illness with the individual and their family. Education is a vital element of the process, ensuring that individuals understand their illness and what they can do to manage it properly.

19. Treatment Planning:

- Once a diagnosis is determined, the following step is to construct a specific treatment plan. This treatment may involve medication, therapy (such as cognitive-behavioral therapy or dialectical behavior therapy), and lifestyle changes targeted at stabilizing mood and preventing relapses.

20. Ongoing Monitoring and Review:

- The diagnostic process doesn't end with a diagnosis; it's a beginning point for continuous care. Regular monitoring and evaluations are crucial to follow the individual's progress, adjust treatment as appropriate, and address any problems or changes in symptoms.

21. Support Network Involvement:

- In many circumstances, involving the support network, including family and friends, can be advantageous. Educating and enlightening loved ones about bipolar disease can help create a more understanding and supportive atmosphere.

22. Crisis Planning:

- Developing a crisis plan is a vital element of the diagnostic procedure. This plan specifies measures to take in the event of a severe mood episode, offering a clear route for getting help and support when needed.

The diagnostic process of bipolar disorder is a complex and comprehensive journey that needs rigorous testing, collaboration, education, and support.

A correct diagnosis is the cornerstone for devising an effective treatment plan and helping individuals manage their disease and lead stable, satisfying lives. It's vital for persons experiencing symptoms of bipolar disorder to seek professional evaluation and care to obtain the help they need.

Chapter 4

<u>TREATMENT OPTIONS</u>

The treatment of bipolar disorder often involves a combination of medication, therapy, and lifestyle improvements to help individuals manage their symptoms and lead stable, satisfying lives. The specific treatment approach can vary depending on the nature and severity of the condition, as well as individual preferences and needs. Let's review these therapy alternatives in detail:

1. Medication:

Medication is a cornerstone of bipolar illness treatment. There are various types of drugs used to stabilize mood and manage symptoms. These include:

- <u>Mood Stabilizers:</u> Mood stabilizers, such as lithium, valproic acid (Depakote), and lamotrigine (Lamictal), are widely recommended to assist in regulating mood and prevent mood swings. Lithium, in particular, has a long history of success in treating bipolar disorder.

- <u>Antipsychotic Medications:</u> Atypical antipsychotic medicines such as aripiprazole (Abilify), olanzapine (Zyprexa), and quetiapine (Seroquel) are typically used to control manic and mixed episodes. Some of these drugs can also be used as mood stabilizers.

- <u>Antidepressants:</u> Antidepressants are infrequently used in the treatment of bipolar disorder, although they are normally taken with caution, often in combination with a mood stabilizer or antipsychotic to prevent triggering manic episodes.

- <u>Antianxiety Medications:</u> Medications like benzodiazepines may be used in the short term to alleviate extreme anxiety or agitation during manic or mixed episodes, but they are generally not suggested for long-term usage due to the risk of addiction.

- <u>Antidepressant-antipsychotic Combinations</u>: Some drugs combine an antidepressant with an antipsychotic to manage depressed symptoms without inducing mania.

- <u>Medication for Sleep:</u> Given the relevance of sleep disruptions in bipolar disorder, some persons may be prescribed sleep aids to assist in regulating their sleep patterns.

- <u>Medicine Adjustments:</u> It's crucial to note that medicine may need to be modified frequently based on an individual's response and changing symptoms. Finding the proper drug and dosage typically entails a trial-and-error process.

2. Psychotherapy (Therapy):

- <u>Cognitive-Behavioral Therapy (CBT)</u>: CBT is an evidence-based therapy that helps patients recognize and change problematic thought patterns and behaviors. It can be effective in treating depression symptoms and boosting coping abilities.

- <u>Dialectical Behavior treatment (DBT)</u>: DBT is a type of cognitive-behavioral treatment that focuses on controlling emotions and interpersonal relationships. It can be particularly beneficial in managing mood instability and impulsive conduct.

- <u>Interpersonal and Social Rhythm Therapy (IPSRT)</u>: IPSRT is aimed to assist individuals in controlling their daily routines, sleep patterns, and managing interpersonal interactions. It has been demonstrated to be useful in reducing relapses in bipolar disorder.

- <u>Family-Focused Therapy (FFT):</u> FFT incorporates family members in the therapy process and focuses on enhancing family communication, lowering stress, and offering support to the individual with bipolar disorder.

- <u>Group Therapy:</u> Group therapy offers a supportive setting where individuals can share experiences, and coping strategies, and learn insights from peers who are also living with bipolar disease.

- <u>Psychoeducation:</u> Education regarding bipolar disorder, its symptoms, and successful self-management skills is a vital part of treatment. It helps individuals to better understand their situation and make educated decisions.

3. Lifestyle Adjustments:
- <u>Regular Sleep Patterns:</u> Establishing and maintaining regular sleep patterns is key in

managing bipolar illness. Disrupted sleep might provoke mood episodes.

- <u>Healthy Diet and Exercise:</u> A balanced diet and regular physical activity contribute to general well-being and can help stabilize mood.

- <u>Stress Management:</u> Learning stress-reduction practices such as mindfulness, meditation, or yoga can help manage stress, which is a known trigger for mood disorders.

- <u>Avoidance of Alcohol and Drugs:</u> Substance misuse can worsen bipolar symptoms and should be avoided. Substance abuse treatment may be necessary if it's a worry.

- <u>Establishing a Supportive Network:</u> Engaging with friends, family, and support groups can provide vital emotional support and encouragement.

- <u>Regular Monitoring:</u> Individuals may benefit from keeping a mood journal to track symptoms and find patterns or triggers.

4. Electroconvulsive Therapy (ECT):

- In severe cases where medicine and therapy are ineffectual or the individual's safety is at stake, electroconvulsive therapy (ECT) may be explored. ECT includes the controlled induction of a seizure to alter brain chemistry. It is normally reserved for serious instances and delivered under anesthesia and muscle relaxants.

5. Hospitalization:

- In cases of severe manic or depressive episodes where the individual is at risk of harm to themselves or others, hospitalization may be necessary to give intense therapy and assure safety.

6. Complementary and Alternative Therapies:

- Some people investigate supplementary and alternative therapies, such as acupuncture, meditation, or herbal remedies, as adjuncts to their primary treatment. It's crucial to examine these alternatives with healthcare providers.

7. Relapse Prevention Strategies:

- As part of bipolar disorder therapy, individuals are often taught relapse prevention methods. These tactics entail identifying early warning signals of mood episodes and making proactive efforts to prevent them from intensifying. This may include lifestyle improvements, medication adjustments, or more therapy sessions as necessary.

8. Medication Adherence:

- Consistent medication adherence is critical for patients with bipolar illness to maintain stability. Healthcare professionals work closely with individuals to select the proper prescription, assess its effectiveness, and manage potential adverse effects. It's vital to follow the specified medication regimen and share any issues with the healthcare professional.

9. Long-Term Management:
- Bipolar disorder is a lifetime condition, and long-term management is required. Regular follow-up meetings with healthcare specialists are necessary to check continuing symptom management and therapy success.

10. Self-Management Skills:
- Education and skill-building are crucial components of treatment. Individuals are taught self-management skills, such as recognizing triggers, controlling stress, and adhering to treatment regimens. These abilities empower individuals to take an active role in their own mental health and well-being.

11. Integrated Care:

- For many individuals, bipolar disorder commonly co-occurs with other problems, such as anxiety or substance use disorders. Integrated care that addresses both the core mood disorder and any co-occurring illnesses is crucial for comprehensive treatment.

12. Personalized Treatment Plans:

- The therapy of bipolar disorder is extremely customized. Each person may have a different combination of mood symptoms and co-occurring illnesses, which necessitates personalized treatment regimens that address their particular requirements and limitations.

13. Support Systems:

- A robust support system, including family, friends, and support groups, plays a crucial role in helping those with bipolar disorder maintain stability and manage obstacles.

Loved ones can provide emotional support and encouragement.

14. Safety Planning:

- Creating a safety plan is a vital element of bipolar illness treatment. This plan describes procedures to take in the event of a crisis, such as a severe mood episode or suicidal thoughts, ensuring that individuals have a clear route for getting help and support.

15. Advocacy and Awareness:

- Many individuals and their families engage in advocacy and awareness activities to eliminate stigma, expand access to treatment, and promote knowledge of bipolar disease within their communities.

Bipolar disease can be tough, but with the correct treatment and support, many persons can attain a great quality of life.

The value of a treatment plan cannot be emphasized, especially when it comes to managing complicated disorders like bipolar disorder. A well-structured and customized treatment plan is necessary for various reasons:

1. Accurate Diagnosis:

A treatment plan begins with a full assessment, which involves a meticulous evaluation of symptoms, medical history, and often the involvement of loved ones. This procedure helps ensure an accurate diagnosis, which is the cornerstone for good treatment.

2. Tailored Approach:

Every individual with bipolar illness experiences the condition differently. A treatment plan is individualized to meet the exact form of bipolar illness, the severity of symptoms, co-occurring conditions, and the individual's unique needs and preferences.

3. Medication Management:

For bipolar disorder, medication is generally a major component of treatment. A treatment plan specifies the choice of drug, dose, and any required modifications. It also offers a regimen for taking medication and assessing its effectiveness.

4. Therapy & Counseling:

A treatment plan often involves multiple forms of therapy, such as cognitive-behavioral therapy (CBT), dialectical behavior therapy (DBT), or interpersonal and social rhythm therapy (IPSRT). These therapies assist patients to learn coping strategies, develop understanding, and manage mood crises.

5. Consistency and Adherence:

Having a structured treatment plan encourages consistency in adhering to medication and therapy appointments. Consistency is essential for stabilizing mood and preventing relapses.

6. Crisis Management:

A well-designed treatment plan includes a crisis management component, outlining steps to take in the event of a severe mood episode or a mental health crisis. This provides a clear roadmap for seeking help and support when needed.

7. Monitoring and Adjustment:

Bipolar disorder can be dynamic, and symptoms may change over time. A treatment plan involves regular monitoring of an individual's progress and adjustments to the plan when necessary. This guarantees that the treatment remains effective and responsive to changing demands.

8. Relapse Prevention:

A good treatment plan incorporates strategies for relapse prevention. By identifying early warning signs of mood episodes, individuals and their healthcare providers can take proactive steps to prevent these episodes from escalating.

9. Holistic Approach:

Bipolar disorder treatment frequently entails lifestyle modifications. The treatment strategy may incorporate advice for regular sleep patterns, a balanced diet, exercise, stress management strategies, and the avoidance of substances like alcohol and narcotics that might increase symptoms.

10. Support Network Involvement:

A treatment plan recognizes the necessity of incorporating a support network, such as family and friends. Education and conversation with loved ones about bipolar disease can create a more understanding and supportive atmosphere.

11. Long-Term Management:

Bipolar disorder is a lifelong condition, and a treatment plan is not a one-time solution. It is a developing roadmap for long-term management that helps patients retain stability and control their illness over time.

12. Self-Empowerment:

A treatment plan informs individuals about their disease, treatment alternatives, and self-management tactics. This encourages individuals to take an active role in their own mental health and well-being.

13. Ongoing Collaboration:

A treatment plan facilitates continuing engagement between individuals and their healthcare professionals. This teamwork ensures that the treatment remains aligned with the individual's changing requirements and goals.

14. Improved Quality of Life:

Ultimately, the objective of a treatment plan is to improve the individual's quality of life. By managing symptoms, minimizing mood episodes, and boosting well-being, a well-executed treatment plan can help patients enjoy stable, fulfilling lives.

In summary, a detailed and tailored treatment plan is a vital tool for managing bipolar disease efficiently. It supports individuals, healthcare professionals, and support networks in adopting an organized and holistic approach to treatment.

With the correct treatment plan, persons with bipolar disorder can limit the impact of mood episodes, reduce relapses, and lead stable and satisfying lives.

Chapter 5

<u>THE ROLE OF THE SUPPORT SYSTEM</u>

Individuals with bipolar disorder typically rely on a strong support system to help them manage their disease and handle the problems it poses. The support system, which often comprises family, friends, and partners, plays a critical role in numerous elements of an individual's experience with bipolar disorder:

1. Emotional Support:

One of the key tasks of the support system is to provide emotional support. Individuals with bipolar disorder often experience strong mood changes, which can be tough to cope with on their own. Having a support network that gives compassion, empathy, and a nonjudgmental attitude can make a tremendous difference in helping individuals cope with these mood variations.

2. Encouragement and Motivation:
Living with bipolar disorder can be tough, and individuals may endure moments of low motivation and self-doubt. A friendly atmosphere can provide encouragement and incentive to persist with treatment programs, attend therapy, and practice self-care.

3. Assistance with Daily Life:
During manic or depressed episodes, individuals may find it challenging to accomplish ordinary duties and responsibilities. The support system can step in to help with practical things like meal preparation, transportation, and childcare, ensuring that the person with bipolar disorder receives essential care.

4. Crisis Intervention:
In certain situations, bipolar disorder can lead to severe mood episodes, self-harm, or suicide ideation. The support system should be well-informed about crisis intervention and know when to seek professional aid or contact emergency services to safeguard the individual's safety.

5. Reducing Stigma and Isolation:
Individuals with bipolar disorder often endure stigma and societal misconceptions regarding their disease. A supportive network can function as a buffer against this stigma, offering acceptance and a sense of belonging that opposes the isolation that sometimes accompanies mental health difficulties.

<u>The Support Network: Family, Friends, and Partners</u>

- <u>Family</u>: Family members often play a significant part in the support system of someone with bipolar disorder. They may be responsible for assistance with medical appointments, medication adherence, and monitoring mood changes. Family support can be crucial in crisis management and maintaining a stable living environment.

- <u>Friends:</u> Friends can offer a particular form of support, generally based on trust, shared experiences, and companionship. Friends can be a source of emotional support, lending a listening ear and creating a social network that can battle feelings of isolation.

- <u>Partners:</u> A romantic partner of someone with bipolar disorder may be the closest and most intimate part of the support network. They can offer emotional support, engage in treatment sessions, and aid with daily activities. Partners may also assist in tracking mood shifts and intervene in crisis circumstances.

The Challenges of Loving Someone with Bipolar Disorder

Loving someone with bipolar disease can be wonderful, but it also comes with particular challenges:

- <u>Mood Swings:</u> The unexpected mood swings associated with bipolar disease can be emotionally taxing for loved ones. Dealing with tremendous highs (mania) and lows (depression) can challenge the patience and strength of the support system.

- <u>Medication and Treatment Compliance:</u> Encouraging and guaranteeing medication and treatment compliance can be tough. Loved ones may need to help manage prescriptions, attend treatment sessions, and monitor adverse effects.

- <u>Crisis Management:</u> Coping with manic or depressed periods and knowing when to intervene can be intimidating. Loved ones typically have the burden of spotting warning signs and seeking expert aid in crises.

- <u>Self-Care and Boundaries:</u> Supporting someone with bipolar disease entails balancing support with self-care. Loved ones must create reasonable limits to prevent caregiving burnout.

The Power of a Supportive Environment

A supportive environment can have a tremendous impact on the well-being and recovery of individuals with bipolar disorder:

- <u>Stability:</u> Consistency and stability in daily living are vital for controlling bipolar disorder. A supportive setting can provide a stable routine, minimizing the likelihood of mood disorders produced by interruptions.

- <u>Reduced Stress:</u> Lowering stress levels is vital for those with bipolar disorder, as stress can increase symptoms. A support network can assist in alleviating stress by sharing responsibilities and offering emotional comfort.

- <u>Enhanced Treatment Outcomes:</u> Individuals with bipolar disorder are more likely to adhere to their treatment regimens when they have a supportive atmosphere that supports and monitors medication and therapy.

- <u>Empowerment:</u> A supportive network can empower individuals by providing them with the confidence and determination to manage their condition efficiently. Feeling understood and appreciated can enhance self-esteem and hope.

- <u>Improved Quality of Life:</u> Ultimately, a supportive environment can boost the overall quality of life for someone with bipolar disorder. With the correct assistance, individuals may lead full lives, create great relationships, and achieve their personal and professional goals.

Effective Communication Techniques

Effective communication is crucial when communicating with someone who has bipolar disorder. It can lead to increased awareness, support, and the ability to navigate the problems that this illness provides. Here are some basic approaches to good communication:

1. <u>Active Listening</u>: Actively listen to what the person with bipolar disorder is saying. Pay attention to their words, tone, and body language. Show that you are genuinely involved and interested in their thoughts and feelings.

2. <u>Utilize "I" Statements</u>: When expressing your personal views or worries, utilize "I" statements to describe your sentiments and

opinions. For example, say, "I feel worried when I see you experiencing mood swings," instead of making accusations.

3. <u>Stay Calm and Patient:</u> Bipolar disorder can lead to high emotions and mood changes. It's vital to remain cool and patient throughout interactions, even when they become challenging. Avoid reacting emotionally to their emotional state.

4. <u>Avoid Blame:</u> Instead of blaming the person for their mood swings or conduct, offer your concern and understanding. Blame can intensify disagreements and make the problem worse.

5. <u>Be plain and Direct:</u> Use plain and straightforward language when discussing crucial subjects. Avoid vague or ambiguous communication, as it might lead to misconceptions.

6. <u>Respect Boundaries:</u> Understand and respect the individual's boundaries and comfort zones for communication. Some people may prefer to discuss their illness and feelings in privacy, while others may be more open in a group situation.

7. <u>Nonverbal Communication:</u> Pay attention to your nonverbal signs. Your body language, facial expressions, and tone of voice can transmit as much information as your words. Ensure your nonverbal communication is encouraging and empathetic.

8. <u>Offer Encouragement:</u> Provide positive praise and encouragement. Let the person know you support their attempts to manage their condition and that you are there to help.

9. <u>Ask Open-Ended Questions:</u> Encourage open discourse by asking open-ended questions that allow thorough responses.

This can help the person communicate their thoughts and feelings more fully.

10. <u>Avoid Judgment:</u> Refrain from making judgments or delivering unsolicited advice. Instead, exhibit understanding and a willingness to assist in identifying solutions.

Listening and Empathy

Listening and practicing empathy are crucial components of effective communication when dealing with bipolar disorder. Here's how you can implement these concepts:

1. <u>Practice Active Listening:</u> Actively listen to the person, and avoid interrupting or planning your response while they are speaking. Give them your complete attention.

2. <u>Show Empathy:</u> Put yourself in the other person's shoes and try to comprehend their perspective. Validate their feelings and

experiences, even if you don't agree with their emotions.

3. <u>Reflect and Validate:</u> Reflect their emotions and experiences to them. For example, you might remark, "It sounds like you're feeling overwhelmed right now. I'm here to support you."

4. <u>Avoid Judgment:</u> Refrain from passing judgment or delivering unsolicited advice. Instead, establish a secure space for the person to discuss their views and feelings without fear of censure.

5. <u>Use Supportive Language:</u> Choose your words carefully to communicate empathy and support. Phrases like "I'm here for you" and "I understand this must be challenging" can be consoling.

6. <u>Respect Their Pace:</u> Recognize that the person may not always be ready to communicate or disclose their feelings.

Respect their speed and give them the space they need when appropriate.

7. <u>Offer Physical Comfort:</u> Sometimes, a simple touch or physical gesture can offer empathy and support. A hug or holding their hand might be reassuring.

8. <u>Stay Non-Judgmental:</u> Even if you don't entirely comprehend their emotions, stay away from judgment and criticism. Remember that their feelings are real, and they are doing their best to control them.

Navigating Mood Swings and Crises

Managing mood swings and crises is one of the most tough aspects of interacting with someone with bipolar disorder. Here are techniques to navigate these situations:

1. <u>Educate Yourself:</u> Gain a complete understanding of bipolar disorder, including its symptoms, triggers, and warning

indications of mood swings. This understanding will help you reply more effectively.

2. <u>Develop a Crisis Plan:</u> Work with the person to build a crisis plan that specifies steps to follow in case of severe mood episodes. Identify healthcare specialists, crisis hotlines, and emergency contacts.

3. <u>Maintain Communication:</u> Even amid mood fluctuations, attempt to maintain open channels of communication. Offer your support and urge them to communicate their feelings. Remember that kids may not always be responsive, but regular communication can help.

4. <u>Set Boundaries:</u> Establish clear boundaries and expectations for behavior during mood episodes. Discuss these boundaries when the person is stable and open to the conversation.

5. <u>Safety First:</u> In times of severe catastrophes, prioritize safety. If the person is a danger to himself or others, get professional help immediately. It's crucial to prioritize safety above all else.

6. <u>Respect Their Coping Techniques:</u> People with bipolar disorder frequently have coping techniques to control mood fluctuations. While some may be unhealthy, it's vital to respect their tactics and, when necessary, push healthier choices.

7. <u>Stay Calm:</u> During a crisis, it's crucial to remain calm and composed. Responding with rage or irritation might aggravate the situation. Offer reassurance and support.

8. <u>Provide Comfort:</u> Simple gestures of comfort, such as giving a blanket, preparing a cup of tea, or sitting quietly with the individual, can be soothing during crises.

9. <u>Seek Professional Help:</u> If mood swings become uncontrolled, or the person is experiencing severe symptoms, don't hesitate to contact a mental health professional or crisis hotline for guidance.

10. <u>Encourage Self-Care:</u> Promote self-care activities that can assist the person in managing their mood and minimize stress. This may involve exercise, relaxation techniques, and maintaining a regular sleep schedule.

Navigating mood swings and crises needs understanding, patience, and a dedication to providing a secure and supportive atmosphere. By adopting these measures, you can play a vital role in helping individuals with bipolar disorder manage their condition and enhance their general well-being.

Chapter 6

<u>COPING AS A COUPLE</u>

Coping in a marriage when one member is dealing with bipolar disorder may be both a tough and rewarding process. This thorough guide addresses the nuances of romantic relationships and bipolar disease, the problems and opportunities that occur, and how couples can develop a successful and supportive partnership.

Bipolar disorder, formerly known as manic-depressive disease, is a mental health condition marked by significant mood swings. These mood fluctuations include periods of mania (elevated mood and vigor) and depression (low mood and energy).

While bipolar disease can pose substantial problems to romantic relationships, it's crucial to remember that persons with this diagnosis can lead full, loving lives with the correct assistance. Let's go more into the intricacies of love relationships with bipolar disorder:

1. Love and Bipolar Disorder:

- Love is not defined by one's mental health status. People with bipolar disorder are capable of experiencing deep, meaningful relationships.

- Romantic partners can offer vital assistance in managing bipolar disorder, and love can be a source of strength and stability.

2. The Impact of Mood Swings:

- Mood swings linked with bipolar disease can have a severe influence on relationships. Partners may observe phases of mania, marked by impulsivity and high energy, and times of depression, characterized by low energy and motivation.

- These mood fluctuations can impair communication, intimacy, and the entire dynamic of the partnership.

3. Communication and Understanding:

- Effective communication is crucial to understanding and supporting a spouse with bipolar disorder.

- Partners should work together to provide an open and nonjudgmental space for discussing symptoms, treatment, and emotional needs.

4. Empathy and Validation:

- Demonstrating empathy and validation is vital. Partners should acknowledge the emotional experiences of the individual with bipolar disorder without judgment.

- Validation can help lessen feelings of loneliness and promote a sense of connection.

Challenges and Opportunities

Romantic relationships with bipolar disease come with unique obstacles, but they also bring potential for growth and resilience. It's vital to address these difficulties openly and work collaboratively to seize the opportunities:

1. Coping with Mood Episodes:

- Manic episodes may involve impulsivity and heightened energy, which can be exhilarating but often unpleasant for relationships.

- Depressive episodes may lead to disengagement, anger, and less intimacy. Partners may need to adapt to variations in mood.

2. Treatment Adherence:

- Encouraging and promoting treatment adherence is a regular difficulty. Medication and therapy are typically crucial components of controlling bipolar disorder.

- Partners can help monitor drug schedules, offer reminders, and participate in therapy sessions when appropriate.

3. Crisis Management:

- Coping with severe mood swings or crises can be emotionally taxing. Partners should have a crisis plan in place, including procedures to take in situations.

- Crisis management typically entails contacting healthcare specialists or crisis hotlines to ensure safety.

4. Stigma and Misconceptions:

- Stigma and misconceptions regarding bipolar disorder can add an added degree of stress. Partners should work collaboratively to dispel these myths and enhance understanding.

- Educational activities help minimize the stigma associated with bipolar disorder within the relationship and the broader community.

5. Self-Care and Boundaries:

- Partners must emphasize self-care and establish healthy limits to minimize caregiving burnout. Caring for oneself allows greater support for the individual with bipolar disorder.

- Open discussions about boundaries and self-care can lead to a healthier partnership dynamic.

6. Resilience and Growth:

- Coping with bipolar disorder can build resilience and personal growth. Partners often become more adaptive, sympathetic, and compassionate through their experiences.

- Overcoming hardships together can build the link and lead to a stronger connection.

<u>Building a Thriving Partnership</u>

A thriving partnership in the context of bipolar disorder is conceivable. With understanding, effort, and a commitment to communication, couples can develop a relationship that supports the well-being and happiness of both partners:

1. Education and Awareness:

- Education about bipolar disorder is the cornerstone for developing a productive collaboration. Both spouses should have a strong understanding of the condition.

- Awareness of the specific symptoms and causes for the individual with bipolar disorder can inform solutions for support and care.

2. Open and Nonjudgmental Communication:

- Create a climate of open and nonjudgmental communication. Partners should feel safe sharing feelings, triggers, and therapy choices.

- Honesty and vulnerability are crucial components of good communication.

3. Mutual Support:

- Both couples require support, and it's crucial to provide mutual encouragement. Supporting each other's well-being helps establish a balanced and healthy partnership.

- Acknowledge that both partners may have their issues and demands.

4. Shared Responsibility:
- Shared responsibility for managing bipolar disorder generates a sense of unity. Partners can collaborate on treatment planning, crisis management, and self-care techniques.

- This shared responsibility might minimize the load on the individual with bipolar disorder.

5. Resilience and Coping Strategies:
- Develop resilience and coping mechanisms as a team. This requires developing productive strategies to navigate mood swings and crises.

- Learning together and progressing through problems can deepen the partnership.

6. Seek Professional Help:
- Professional support is available for couples managing bipolar disorder. Couples therapy can give a forum for shared talks and solutions for managing the disease.

- Seeking treatment doesn't show weakness but rather a dedication to the relationship's well-being.

7. Celebrate Achievements:
- Celebrate victories, no matter how minor. Recognize improvements and accomplishments in controlling bipolar disorder.

- Positive praise can drive continuous effort and deepen the connection.

8. Encourage Independence:
- Encourage independence and autonomy for the individual with bipolar disorder. A

good partnership entails acknowledging each person's originality and self-sufficiency.

- Balance support with the possibility for personal progress.

9. Reduce Stigma Together:
- Engage in initiatives to remove stigma and increase understanding. By confronting stereotypes and fighting for mental health, couples can contribute to a more caring and compassionate community.

- Together, couples can be ambassadors of empathy and awareness.

10. Prioritize Self-Care:
- Prioritize self-care individually and as a pair. Recognize that caring for yourself offers better support for your partner and the relationship as a whole.

- Self-care might include maintaining personal hobbies, receiving emotional support from friends, and practicing relaxation techniques.

With understanding, empathy, and dedication to each other, couples can build a loving and supportive atmosphere that encourages them to thrive in the face of bipolar disease.

Chapter 7

<u>SELF-CARE FOR CAREGIVERS</u>

Self-care for caregivers is a vital component of giving effective and sustainable support to individuals with various health conditions, including mental health challenges like bipolar illness. Caregivers typically focus on the well-being of their loved ones but may disregard their own needs.

Caring for someone with bipolar disorder can be emotionally and physically draining. To be a good caregiver, it is vital to prioritize self-care. Here's why self-care is essential:

1. Maintain Your Well-being:
- By taking care of your own needs, you can maintain your physical and mental health. Self-care helps prevent caregiver burnout, exhaustion, and health issues.

2. Sustain Your Ability to Care:

- Proper self-care ensures you can provide consistent and high-quality care to your loved one. When you are physically and mentally well, you are better equipped to support their needs.

3. Reduce Stress:

- Caregiving can be stressful, and long-term stress can take a toll on your health. Self-care practices can help reduce stress and promote relaxation.

4. Enhance Resilience:

- Self-care fosters emotional resilience, helping you cope with the emotional challenges that can arise in your role as a caregiver.

5. Strengthen the Caregiver-Patient Relationship:

- When you are well and balanced, you are more likely to have a positive and helpful relationship with the person you are caring for.

Self-Care Strategies for Caregivers

Self-care comprises several behaviors and tactics that address physical, emotional, and mental well-being. Consider these techniques to include self-care in your life as a caregiver:

1. Prioritize Physical Health:

- Ensure you receive regular exercise, maintain a balanced diet, and get adequate sleep. Physical well-being is the foundation of all other aspects of self-care.

- Schedule regular check-ups with your healthcare professional to monitor your health.

2. Set Boundaries:

- Establish clear limits in your caregiving position. Define what you can and cannot do and explain these boundaries to the individual you are caring for and your support network.

- Say no when necessary, and don't overcommit or take on more duties than you can handle.

3. Take Breaks:
- Regularly schedule short breaks and extended periods of respite from caregiving. These breaks allow you to rest, recover, and focus on your personal needs.

4. Seek Emotional Support:
- Connect with friends, family, or support groups. Share your experiences, feelings, and challenges with others who understand your job as a caregiver.

- Consider obtaining professional counseling or therapy if you notice that your emotional well-being is adversely impaired.

5. Practice Mindfulness and Relaxation Techniques:
- Engage in mindfulness activities, meditation, or deep breathing to reduce stress and maintain emotional equilibrium.

- Allocate time for relaxation and leisure activities that bring you joy and calm.

6. Maintain Personal Interests:
- Continue to engage in activities and interests that you are enthusiastic about. Pursuing personal interests outside of parenting helps you keep your identity.

7. Accept Help:
- Don't hesitate to accept help from others. Let family and friends assist with caregiving activities or domestic chores to ease your load.

8. Stay Informed:

- Educate yourself about the condition of the person you are caring for. Understanding their needs and triggers might help you give better care and lessen stress.

9. Time Management:

- Efficiently manage your time by setting a timetable or habit. This might help you manage caring with personal and business duties.

10. Maintain a Support Network:

- Nurture a support network of friends and family who may supply aid and emotional support when needed.

<u>Benefits of Self-Care for Caregivers</u>

Prioritizing self-care as a caregiver provides numerous key benefits:

1. Improved Well-being:

- Self-care techniques strengthen your physical and emotional health, ensuring you remain in good shape to provide care.

2. Reduced Stress and Burnout:

- Managing stress via self-care minimizes the likelihood of caregiver burnout, tiredness, and mental health difficulties.

3. Enhanced Resilience:

- Self-care fosters emotional resilience, allowing you to better cope with the emotional challenges that come with caregiving.

4. Better Caregiving:

- Taking care of yourself ensures you can provide consistent and high-quality care to your loved one.

5. Strengthened Relationships:

- A well-balanced caregiver is more likely to have positive and supportive connections with the individuals they care for and with their support network.

6. Increased Energy and Motivation:

- Engaging in self-care techniques can enhance your energy levels and motivation, making you more effective in your caregiving position.

7. Personal Fulfillment:

- Pursuing personal interests and self-care activities outside of caregiving can bring personal fulfillment and a feeling of individual identity.

Self-Care as a Continuous Practice

Self-care is not a one-time event but an ongoing practice. As a caregiver, it's crucial to incorporate self-care into your daily routine and make it a priority. Be adaptive in your self-care tactics and alter them as needed to suit your changing circumstances and requirements.

Remember that self-care is not selfish; it's a crucial element of being a competent and compassionate caregiver. Prioritizing your well-being enables you to provide better support to your loved one and maintain your own physical and mental well. It's an investment in your ability to continue and prosper in your role as a caregiver.

www.ingramcontent.com/pod-product-compliance
Lightning Source LLC
Chambersburg PA
CBHW050837260726
48660CB00006B/2284